Raising Remarkable Kids: A Guide To Developing Social Skills For Children

Barley Nicola

Published by Barley Nicola, 2024.

RAISING REMARKABLE KIDS: A GUIDE TO DEVELOPING SOCIAL SKILLS FOR CHILDREN

First edition. April 2, 2024.

Copyright © 2024 Barley Nicola.

ISBN: 979-8224964062

Written by Barley Nicola.

Table of Contents

• • • •

- IMPORTANCE OF SOCIAL Skills in Children

Social skills play a crucial role in the development of children as they navigate the complex social environment around them. These skills encompass a range of abilities that allow individuals to interact effectively with others, including communication, empathy, cooperation, and conflict resolution. Developing strong social skills from a young age is essential for a child's overall well-being and success in life.

One of the key reasons why social skills are important for children is their impact on interpersonal relationships. The ability to communicate effectively, understand others' perspectives, and work collaboratively with others is essential for building strong and meaningful connections with family, friends, and peers. Children who possess strong social skills are more likely to form positive relationships, experience less conflict, and have a sense of belonging and acceptance in social groups.

In addition to fostering positive relationships, social skills also play a critical role in academic achievement. Research has shown that children with strong social skills are better able to focus on their studies, work well with teachers and peers, and participate actively in classroom discussions and group projects. These children are also more likely to seek help when needed, engage in productive study habits, and persevere through challenges, leading to improved academic performance and overall success in school.

Furthermore, developing social skills in children can have a significant impact on their emotional well-being and mental health. Children who lack social skills may struggle with feelings of loneliness, isolation, and low self-esteem, which can contribute to anxiety, depression, and other mental health issues. On the other hand, children who possess strong social skills are more likely to have positive self-esteem, feel connected to others, and have the resilience to cope with stress and adversity.

Another important aspect of social skills is their role in promoting prosocial behavior and empathy in children. By understanding and valuing the perspectives and feelings of others, children learn to be kind, compassionate, and considerate in their interactions with others. These qualities are essential for building a compassionate and inclusive society, where individuals are able to work together towards common goals, resolve conflicts peacefully, and support one another in times of need.

It is important for parents, educators, and caregivers to actively support and cultivate the development of social skills in children. This can be achieved through a variety of strategies, such as modeling positive social behaviors, providing opportunities for children to practice and strengthen their social skills, and offering guidance and feedback to help them navigate social situations effectively. By prioritizing the development of social skills in children, we can help them build the foundation for a fulfilling and successful life, both academically and personally. By fostering the development of social skills in children, we can help them build positive relationships, succeed academically, promote emotional well-being, and cultivate empathy and prosocial behavior. It is crucial for parents, educators, and caregivers to prioritize the development of social skills in children and provide them with the support and guidance they need to navigate the social world effectively. By doing so, we can help children thrive and reach their full potential as individuals and members of society.

• • • •

- DEFINITION OF SOCIAL Skills

Social skills are a crucial component of human interaction and communication in both personal and professional settings. They refer to the ability to effectively navigate social situations, communicate with others, and build relationships. Social skills encompass a range of behaviors and attitudes that allow individuals to interact with others in a positive and productive manner. These skills are essential for building strong relationships, resolving conflicts, and collaborating with others to achieve common goals.

One key aspect of social skills is effective communication. This includes the ability to express oneself clearly and confidently, listen actively and attentively, and adapt communication style to different situations and individuals. Effective communication is not only about speaking and listening but also about using nonverbal cues such as body language, facial expressions, and gestures to convey messages and understand others' emotions and intentions. Being a good communicator requires empathy, understanding, and the ability to communicate in a way that is respectful, empathetic, and understanding of others' perspectives.

Another important aspect of social skills is the ability to build and maintain relationships. This involves establishing rapport, showing interest in others, and fostering trust and respect. Building relationships requires individuals to be attentive, genuine, and responsive to others' needs and feelings. Maintaining relationships involves ongoing communication, support, and a willingness to compromise and resolve conflicts. Strong relationships are built on trust, mutual respect, and open communication, and individuals with strong social skills are able to navigate complex social dynamics and handle interpersonal challenges effectively.

In addition to communication and relationship-building, social skills also include self-awareness and self-regulation. Self-awareness involves recognizing one's own emotions, thoughts, and behaviors, and understanding how they impact oneself and others. Self-regulation involves managing emotions, controlling impulses, and responding to situations in a constructive and appropriate manner. Individuals with strong self-awareness and self-regulation skills are better able to handle stress, conflict, and difficult situations, and are more likely to make thoughtful decisions and act with integrity and compassion.

Social skills are essential for success in both personal and professional life. In personal relationships, strong social skills enable individuals to form meaningful connections, build trust and intimacy, and navigate conflicts and challenges with grace and empathy. In professional settings, social skills are essential for communication, collaboration, leadership, and team building. Individuals with strong social skills are able to build strong networks, influence others, and achieve common goals through effective communication and collaboration. Additionally, social skills are key to navigating workplace dynamics, resolving conflicts, and building a positive and inclusive work environment. Individuals with strong social skills are able to navigate social situations with ease, build strong relationships, and collaborate effectively with others. Social skills involve effective communication, relationship-building, self-awareness, and self-regulation, and are essential for success in both personal and professional life. By developing and honing their social skills, individuals can improve their interpersonal relationships, enhance their communication abilities, and achieve greater success and fulfillment in all areas of their lives.

- Types of Social Skills

Social skills refer to the abilities that allow individuals to interact and communicate effectively with others in various social situations. These skills are essential for building and maintaining relationships, as well as for navigating the complexities of social interactions. There are several different types of social skills that individuals can develop and cultivate over time.

One type of social skill is communication skills, which involve the ability to convey thoughts, feelings, and information clearly and effectively to others. This includes both verbal and nonverbal communication, such as using words, tone of voice, facial expressions, and body language to express oneself. Effective communication skills are critical for expressing ideas, emotions, and needs, as well as for listening and understanding others.

Another important type of social skill is interpersonal skills, which involve the ability to interact and connect with others on a personal level. This includes qualities such as empathy, understanding, and respect for others, as well as the ability to build rapport, establish trust, and resolve conflicts in a positive and constructive manner. Interpersonal skills are essential for developing and maintaining healthy relationships, as well as for collaborating and working effectively with others.

In addition to communication and interpersonal skills, there are also social skills that are specific to different social situations and contexts. For example, there are social skills for formal settings, such as professional networking events or business meetings, which may require a different set of communication and interpersonal skills compared to informal social interactions, such as social gatherings or casual conversations with friends.

Some other types of social skills include assertiveness skills, which involve the ability to express oneself and assert one's needs and boundaries in a clear and respectful manner, as well as conflict resolution skills, which involve the ability to manage and resolve conflicts in a positive and constructive way. These skills are important for navigating challenging and emotionally charged situations, as well as for building self-confidence and self-esteem. By cultivating communication, interpersonal, assertiveness, and conflict resolution skills, individuals can enhance their ability to connect with others, build and maintain relationships, and navigate social situations with confidence and ease. Social skills are not only important for personal relationships but also for professional success, as they are critical for effective communication, teamwork, and leadership in the workplace. By investing time and effort into developing social skills, individuals can enhance their social intelligence and emotional intelligence, leading to greater personal and professional growth and success.

. . . .

- VERBAL COMMUNICATION

Verbal communication is a crucial aspect of human interaction, serving as the primary mode through which individuals convey thoughts, ideas, emotions, and information to one another. It encompasses the spoken word, as well as non-verbal cues such as tone of voice, facial expressions, and body language. Effective verbal communication is essential in both personal and professional settings, as it plays a key role in building relationships, fostering understanding, and resolving conflicts.

One of the most important aspects of verbal communication is clarity. Clear and concise communication ensures that messages are accurately conveyed and understood by all parties involved. This involves using simple and straightforward language, avoiding jargon or technical terms that may be confusing to others. Additionally, being mindful of the tone and volume of one's voice can also enhance clarity in communication. A calm and neutral tone can help prevent misunderstandings or misinterpretations, while maintaining an appropriate volume ensures that all parties can hear and comprehend the message being communicated.

Another key aspect of verbal communication is active listening. Active listening involves paying attention to the speaker, making eye contact, nodding or providing verbal affirmations, and asking clarifying questions to demonstrate understanding. By actively listening, individuals show respect for the speaker and signal their willingness to engage in meaningful dialogue. This practice not only enhances communication effectiveness but also helps build rapport and trust between individuals.

In addition to clarity and active listening, effective verbal communication also involves empathy and emotional intelligence. Empathy is the ability to understand and share the emotions of others, while emotional intelligence refers to the ability to recognize and manage one's own emotions as well as those of others. Both empathy and emotional intelligence are crucial in fostering open and honest communication, as they enable individuals to connect on a deeper level and navigate sensitive or difficult conversations with tact and sensitivity.

Furthermore, cultural awareness and sensitivity are essential components of effective verbal communication, particularly in today's diverse and globalized world. Different cultures have unique communication styles, norms, and taboos, which can impact how messages are interpreted and received. By being mindful of cultural differences and adapting one's communication style accordingly, individuals can avoid misunderstandings and foster cross-cultural understanding and cooperation.

Lastly, feedback and reflection are important tools for improving verbal communication skills. Seeking feedback from others can provide valuable insights into one's communication style, strengths, and areas for improvement. Reflecting on past interactions and identifying patterns or recurring challenges can also help individuals fine-tune their communication skills and become more effective communicators over time. By honing skills such as clarity, active listening, empathy, emotional intelligence, cultural awareness, and feedback, individuals can enhance their verbal communication skills and build stronger connections with others. Effective verbal communication is a lifelong journey of learning and growth, but with practice and dedication, anyone can become a more skilled and impactful communicator.

- Nonverbal Communication

Nonverbal communication is a vital aspect of human interaction that encompasses a wide range of behaviors and cues. Unlike verbal communication, which relies on words and language, nonverbal communication includes gestures, facial expressions, body language, tone of voice, eye contact, and other subtle cues that convey meaning and emotion. This form of communication is believed to make up the majority of our daily interactions, with some studies suggesting that up to 93% of communication is nonverbal. Understanding and interpreting nonverbal cues is crucial in making sense of social interactions, as they can often convey more information than words alone.

One of the key aspects of nonverbal communication is body language. Our bodies are constantly sending signals about our thoughts, feelings, and intentions, even when we are not consciously aware of it. For example, crossed arms and a furrowed brow might indicate defensiveness or disagreement, while open body posture and a smile convey openness and friendliness. By paying attention to these cues, we can gain valuable insights into the thoughts and emotions of others, allowing us to adjust our own behavior accordingly.

Facial expressions are another important component of nonverbal communication. The human face is incredibly expressive, capable of conveying a wide range of emotions from happiness and excitement to anger and sadness. Microexpressions, which are fleeting facial expressions that last for just a fraction of a second, can provide key insights into a person's true feelings, even when they are trying to hide them. Learning to read facial expressions can help us better understand the emotions of others and respond empathetically.

Eye contact is also a significant aspect of nonverbal communication. In many cultures, maintaining eye contact is seen as a sign of respect, interest, and attentiveness, while avoiding eye contact can be interpreted as dishonesty, discomfort, or shyness. Eye contact can convey feelings of intimacy, power dynamics, and emotional connection, making it an important tool in establishing rapport with others. Being mindful of our own eye contact behavior and interpreting the eye contact of others can help us navigate social interactions more effectively.

Tone of voice is yet another element of nonverbal communication that can greatly impact how our messages are perceived. The way we speak, the pitch, volume, and rhythm of our voices, can all convey meaning and emotion. A warm, friendly tone can make our words sound more sincere and engaging, while a harsh or monotonous tone can create distance and misunderstanding. By paying attention to our tone of voice and the tone of others, we can fine-tune our communication skills to better convey our intended message.

Nonverbal communication plays a crucial role in both personal and professional relationships. In the workplace, understanding nonverbal cues can help us navigate complex social dynamics, build trust with colleagues, and convey professionalism and confidence. For example, using appropriate hand gestures and maintaining eye contact during a presentation can help convey competence and credibility to an audience. In interpersonal relationships, nonverbal cues can help us express empathy, establish rapport, and build intimacy with others. By being attentive to nonverbal signals, we can deepen our connections with others and enhance our overall communication effectiveness. Understanding and interpreting nonverbal cues can greatly enhance our ability to communicate effectively, build relationships, and navigate social situations with ease. By paying attention to body language, facial expressions, eye contact, tone of voice, and other nonverbal cues, we can gain valuable insights into the thoughts and emotions of others, improve our own communication skills, and foster stronger interpersonal connections. Ultimately, mastering the art of nonverbal communication is a valuable skill that can benefit us in both our personal and professional lives.

. . . .

- UNDERSTANDING OTHERS' Emotions

Understanding others' emotions is a crucial aspect of effective communication and building strong relationships. By being able to empathize with and recognize the emotions of those around us, we can better respond to their needs, build trust, and foster connections. In this discussion, we will explore the importance of emotional intelligence in understanding others' emotions, the factors that influence our ability to empathize, and practical strategies for improving our empathetic skills.

Emotional intelligence, often referred to as EQ, is the ability to recognize, understand, and manage our own emotions, as well as the emotions of others. It involves skills such as empathy, self-awareness, and social awareness, which are essential for navigating social interactions and interpersonal relationships. Understanding others' emotions requires us to be attuned to nonverbal cues such as facial expressions, body language, and tone of voice, as well as contextual factors such as cultural norms and past experiences. By developing our emotional intelligence, we can increase our capacity to empathize with others and respond sensitively to their needs.

There are several factors that influence our ability to understand others' emotions, including our upbringing, personality traits, and life experiences. For example, individuals who were raised in environments where emotions were not openly discussed or validated may struggle to empathize with others and express their own emotions. Similarly, individuals with certain personality traits, such as high levels of introversion or neuroticism, may find it challenging to connect emotionally with others. Life experiences such as trauma, loss, or conflict can also impact our ability to empathize, as they may cause us to close off emotionally or become defensive in response to others' emotions.

Despite these challenges, there are practical strategies that we can adopt to improve our ability to understand others' emotions. One such strategy is active listening, which involves paying close attention to what others are saying and expressing empathy through verbal and nonverbal cues. By demonstrating that we are fully present and engaged in the conversation, we can convey our understanding and support for the other person's emotions. Another strategy is perspective-taking, which involves putting ourselves in the shoes of others and imagining how they might be feeling in a given situation. By considering the perspectives and emotions of others, we can gain a deeper understanding of their experiences and respond more effectively to their needs.

In addition to these strategies, practicing mindfulness and self-regulation can also help us improve our empathetic skills. Mindfulness involves being fully present in the moment and observing our thoughts, emotions, and bodily sensations without judgment. By cultivating self-awareness through mindfulness practices such as meditation and deep breathing, we can become more attuned to our own emotions and better able to regulate them in response to others. Self-regulation, on the other hand, involves managing our impulses and reactions in order to respond more skillfully to challenging situations. By developing our self-regulation skills, we can avoid reacting impulsively or defensively to others' emotions and instead respond with empathy and compassion. By developing our empathy, self-awareness, and social awareness, we can enhance our ability to connect with others, communicate effectively, and navigate interpersonal conflicts. By practicing active listening, perspective-taking, mindfulness, and self-regulation, we can improve our empathetic skills and become better at recognizing and responding to the emotions of those around us. Ultimately, by fostering a culture of empathy and understanding in our interactions with others, we can create more compassionate, supportive, and harmonious relationships in our personal and professional lives.

- Practicing Empathetic Responses

Empathy is a crucial skill that plays a significant role in our interpersonal relationships, whether personal or professional. It involves understanding and sharing the feelings of others, and responding to them in a supportive and compassionate way. Practicing empathetic responses is essential for building and maintaining healthy relationships, as it fosters trust, understanding, and mutual respect between individuals.

One key aspect of practicing empathetic responses is active listening. Active listening involves fully engaging with the speaker and demonstrating that you are paying attention to their words, feelings, and body language. By giving the speaker your full attention and making an effort to understand their perspective, you can show that you care about their emotions and experiences. This can help the speaker feel heard and validated, which can strengthen your bond and improve communication between you.

Another important element of practicing empathetic responses is acknowledging and validating the speaker's feelings. When someone shares their emotions with you, it is important to acknowledge their feelings and let them know that you understand and empathize with what they are going through. By validating their emotions, you can show that you are present and supportive, and that you care about their well-being. This can create a safe space for the speaker to express themselves and can help them feel understood and accepted.

In addition to active listening and validating emotions, practicing empathetic responses also involves showing empathy through your words and actions. This can include offering words of encouragement, expressing sympathy, or providing practical support to help the speaker feel better. By responding empathetically, you can demonstrate your compassion and understanding, and show that you are willing to help and support the speaker in any way you can. This can help strengthen your relationship and build trust between you, as the speaker will feel valued and cared for.

Furthermore, practicing empathetic responses requires being mindful of your own biases and assumptions. It is important to approach each interaction with an open mind and a willingness to learn and grow. By recognizing and challenging your own biases, you can avoid making judgments or assumptions about the speaker and can create a more inclusive and welcoming space for dialogue. This can help build trust and understanding between you and the speaker, as they will feel respected and valued for who they are. By actively listening, validating emotions, and showing empathy through your words and actions, you can create a supportive and compassionate environment for those around you. By being mindful of your own biases and assumptions, you can foster understanding and mutual respect, and build stronger connections with the people in your life. So, let us all strive to practice empathetic responses in our interactions, and create a more empathetic and understanding world for ourselves and others.

Chapter 5: Developing Conflict Resolution Skills

• • • •

- STRATEGIES FOR RESOLVING Conflicts

Conflicts are a natural part of human interactions and can arise in various situations, from disagreements in the workplace to disputes in personal relationships. It is important to address conflicts promptly and effectively to prevent them from escalating and causing further harm to individuals and relationships. There are several strategies that can be employed to resolve conflicts in a constructive and productive manner.

One strategy for resolving conflicts is through effective communication. Communication is key in any conflict resolution process, as it allows parties involved to express their thoughts, feelings, and concerns in a clear and respectful manner. Active listening is an important component of effective communication, as it involves truly understanding the other person's perspective and validating their feelings. By listening actively and empathetically, individuals can gain a better understanding of the root causes of the conflict and work towards finding a mutually agreeable solution.

Another important strategy for resolving conflicts is through negotiation and compromise. In many conflicts, there is often a need for both parties to give a little in order to reach a resolution that satisfies everyone involved. Negotiation involves finding common ground and exploring potential solutions that address the needs and interests of both parties. Compromise may be necessary in some cases, where individuals must be willing to make concessions in order to reach a mutually beneficial agreement. By approaching conflicts with a spirit of compromise and flexibility, parties can often find creative solutions that meet everyone's needs.

Collaboration is another effective strategy for resolving conflicts. Collaboration involves working together towards a common goal or solution, rather than approaching the conflict as a win-lose situation. By collaborating with the other party or parties involved, individuals can tap into the collective knowledge, skills, and resources of all parties to find a more sustainable and long-lasting resolution. Collaboration fosters a sense of teamwork and

13

partnership, which can help build trust and strengthen relationships even in the face of conflict. It also encourages individuals to consider the bigger picture and focus on finding solutions that benefit everyone involved.

Mediation is a valuable strategy for resolving conflicts, especially in situations where communication has broken down or emotions are running high. Mediation involves bringing in a neutral third party to facilitate discussions and help parties find common ground. The mediator acts as a facilitator, guiding the conversation and encouraging parties to listen to each other and explore potential solutions. By providing a safe and structured environment for communication, mediation can help parties break through impasses and find mutually agreeable resolutions. Mediation is often used in workplace conflicts, family disputes, and community disagreements, and can be a powerful tool for resolving conflicts peacefully and constructively.

Conflict resolution strategies can also benefit from the use of problem-solving techniques. Problem-solving involves approaching conflicts as challenges that can be overcome through creativity, critical thinking, and collaboration. By identifying the underlying issues causing the conflict and brainstorming potential solutions, individuals can work together to find innovative ways to address the conflict and move towards a resolution. Problem-solving techniques can help parties focus on the facts and interests driving the conflict, rather than getting stuck in personal or emotional dynamics. By approaching conflicts with a problem-solving mindset, individuals can work together to find practical and sustainable solutions that meet everyone's needs. It is important to address conflicts promptly and effectively to prevent them from escalating and causing further harm to individuals and relationships. By employing strategies such as effective communication, negotiation and compromise, collaboration, mediation, and problem-solving, parties can work together to find constructive and productive resolutions to conflicts. By approaching conflicts with openness, empathy, and a willingness to listen and compromise, individuals can build stronger relationships, enhance communication, and create a more harmonious and peaceful environment for everyone involved.

- Teaching Kids How to Negotiate

Negotiation is an essential skill that can benefit children throughout their lives. Whether they are negotiating with their classmates on where to play during recess or negotiating with their future employers for a higher salary, the ability to negotiate effectively can greatly enhance their success. Teaching children how to negotiate not only helps them in their interpersonal relationships, but also teaches them important problem-solving and communication skills that will serve them well in any future endeavor.

One important aspect of negotiating is the ability to listen and understand the other party's perspective. Children often struggle with this, as they can be self-centered and focused on their own needs and desires. By teaching them to actively listen and empathize with the other party, children can learn to find common ground and work towards a mutually beneficial solution. Encouraging children to ask questions and show genuine interest in the other party's needs can help them develop better interpersonal skills and create stronger relationships.

Another key component of negotiation is the ability to communicate effectively. Children need to learn how to clearly articulate their wants and needs, as well as actively listen to the wants and needs of the other party. Teaching children to use "I" statements, express their emotions in a healthy way, and practice assertive communication can help them become more confident negotiators. By practicing these communication skills in role-playing scenarios or real-life situations, children can develop the confidence and ability to negotiate effectively in a variety of settings.

It is also important to teach children the value of compromise and flexibility in negotiations. In order to reach a mutually beneficial solution, both parties may need to make concessions and find common ground. By demonstrating the importance of compromise and flexibility in negotiations, parents and educators can help children understand that it is not always possible to get everything they want, but that finding a middle ground can lead to a more successful outcome. Encouraging children to brainstorm multiple solutions and consider the needs of both parties can help them develop a more open-minded and collaborative approach to negotiation.

Furthermore, teaching children how to negotiate can also help them develop problem-solving skills. Negotiations often require creative thinking and the ability to find innovative solutions to complex problems. By encouraging children to think outside the box and explore different options, parents and educators can help them develop their critical thinking and problem-solving skills. Teaching children to consider multiple perspectives, brainstorm creative solutions, and evaluate the pros and cons of different options can help them become more effective problem-solvers and negotiators. By developing their listening, communication, compromise, and problem-solving skills, children can learn to negotiate effectively in a variety of situations. By providing them with opportunities to practice negotiating in a safe and supportive environment, parents and educators can help children build the confidence and skills they need to succeed in their personal and professional lives. With the right guidance and support, children can develop into skilled and confident negotiators who are able to navigate the complexities of the modern world with ease.

. . . .

- TIPS FOR MAKING FRIENDS

Making friends is an essential aspect of human social interaction and can greatly enhance our overall well-being and quality of life. However, for some people, the process of making friends can be challenging or intimidating. Fortunately, there are several tips and strategies that can help individuals navigate the complexities of building and maintaining friendships.

One of the most important tips for making friends is to be yourself. Authenticity is key when it comes to forming meaningful connections with others. Trying to be someone you're not in order to fit in or impress others will only lead to superficial relationships that are unlikely to stand the test of time. Instead, embrace who you are and be confident in your own skin. Showcasing your true personality and interests will attract like-minded individuals who appreciate you for who you are.

Another important tip for making friends is to put yourself out there and be proactive in social situations. While it may be tempting to wait for others to initiate conversations or invitations, taking the first step can often lead to the creation of new friendships. Joining clubs, classes, or community groups that align with your interests can provide a natural opportunity to meet new people and establish connections. Additionally, attending social events or gatherings can help you expand your social circle and meet potential friends.

Building strong friendships requires invest time and effort. It's important to prioritize your relationships and make time for meaningful interactions with your friends. This may involve scheduling regular catch-ups, engaging in shared activities or hobbies, or simply staying in touch through calls or messages. By demonstrating genuine care and support for your friends, you can cultivate trust and deepen your bond over time.

Communication plays a crucial role in the development of friendships. Being an active listener and showing empathy towards others can foster a sense of connection and understanding. When engaging in conversations, make an effort to ask questions, listen attentively, and show genuine interest in what the other person has to say. By demonstrating empathy and understanding, you can create a safe and supportive environment for open communication and the sharing of thoughts and feelings.

In order to make friends, it's important to be open-minded and willing to step out of your comfort zone. Embracing diversity and accepting differences can enrich your social interactions and broaden your perspective. Making an effort to connect with individuals from different backgrounds, cultures, or interests can offer new insights and experiences that can strengthen your friendships. By being open and receptive to new experiences and perspectives, you can expand your social network and create meaningful connections with a diverse range of people.

Maintaining a positive attitude can also play a significant role in making friends. Approaching social interactions with optimism, confidence, and a friendly demeanor can make you more approachable and likable to others. By exuding positivity and warmth, you can create a welcoming and inviting atmosphere that encourages others to engage with you. Additionally, being supportive, encouraging, and uplifting towards your friends can help strengthen your relationships and foster a sense of mutual respect and appreciation. By being authentic, proactive, communicative, open-minded, and positive, you can navigate the complexities of building and maintaining friendships with confidence and ease. Remember to invest time and effort in your relationships, prioritize meaningful interactions, and demonstrate care and support towards your friends. By following these tips and strategies, you can create genuine connections with others and cultivate lasting friendships that enrich your life and bring joy and fulfillment.

- Dealing with Peer Pressure

Peer pressure can be defined as the influence exerted by a peer group on individuals to conform to the group's norms, attitudes, and behaviors. It is a common phenomenon that is experienced by individuals of all ages, but is particularly prevalent during adolescence. During this time, individuals are more likely to seek approval and acceptance from their peers, and may engage in risky behaviors or make decisions that they would not normally make in order to fit in with their social group.

Dealing with peer pressure can be a challenging task, as it can be difficult to resist the influence of others, especially when the pressure is coming from close friends or individuals we admire. However, it is important to remember that succumbing to peer pressure can have negative consequences, both in the short term and in the long term. It is therefore essential to develop strategies to help manage peer pressure effectively and make decisions that align with our own values and beliefs.

One of the first steps in dealing with peer pressure is to be aware of the influence that our peers have on us and to recognize when we are being pressured to do something that we are not comfortable with. This can be achieved by reflecting on our values and beliefs, and considering whether the behavior that is being encouraged aligns with our own principles. It is also important to be mindful of the potential consequences of giving in to peer pressure, and to consider whether the short-term gain of conforming to the group is worth the long-term cost of compromising our integrity.

Another important aspect of dealing with peer pressure is to be assertive and confident in our own decisions and choices. This involves being able to say no to peer pressure in a clear and respectful manner, without feeling the need to justify or explain our decision. It is also important to surround ourselves with individuals who support and respect our choices, and to seek out positive influences that align with our own values and beliefs.

In addition to being assertive, it is also important to communicate effectively with our peers about our boundaries and limits. This can involve setting clear expectations with our friends and expressing our discomfort or disapproval when we are being pressured to do something that goes against our values. By being honest and open with our peers, we can build stronger relationships based on mutual respect and understanding, and avoid the negative consequences of succumbing to peer pressure.

To terminate, it is important to remember that it is okay to be different and to have our own opinions and beliefs. It is important to be true to ourselves and to make decisions that reflect who we are as individuals, rather than conforming to the expectations of others. By staying true to our values and beliefs, we can build confidence in ourselves and resist the pressure to conform to the group, ultimately leading to a greater sense of self-respect and self-esteem. By developing these strategies and skills, we can build stronger relationships with our peers, enhance our self-esteem, and navigate the challenges of peer pressure in a healthy and positive way.

. . . .

- ENCOURAGING SELF-CONFIDENCE

Self-confidence is a crucial aspect of success in both personal and professional realms. It is the belief in one's abilities and worth, leading to a positive self-image and the courage to take risks and pursue one's goals. Encouraging self-confidence in individuals is essential for their overall well-being and fulfillment. By fostering a strong sense of self-belief, individuals are more likely to overcome challenges, adapt to change, and achieve their full potential.

There are several strategies that can be implemented to encourage self-confidence in individuals. One of the most effective ways is through positive reinforcement and validation. By acknowledging and affirming the achievements and strengths of individuals, they are more likely to develop a positive self-image and belief in their abilities. This can be done through praise, constructive feedback, and recognition of their efforts. Additionally, providing opportunities for individuals to showcase their talents and skills can further boost their confidence and self-esteem.

Another important strategy for encouraging self-confidence is through setting realistic goals and providing the support needed to achieve them. Setting achievable goals allows individuals to experience success and build confidence in their abilities. It is important to break down larger goals into smaller, manageable tasks to prevent individuals from feeling overwhelmed or discouraged. Providing encouragement, guidance, and resources to support individuals in reaching their goals can help them develop the confidence needed to tackle challenges and take on new opportunities.

In addition to setting goals, it is important to encourage individuals to step outside of their comfort zones and take risks. Facing fears and trying new experiences can help individuals build resilience and self-confidence. When individuals are willing to take on challenges and confront their fears, they learn that they are capable of overcoming obstacles and thriving in new situations. Encouraging individuals to push themselves beyond their limits and embrace growth opportunities can lead to increased self-confidence and personal growth.

Building self-confidence also requires fostering a positive and supportive environment. Creating a culture of encouragement and empowerment can help individuals feel valued, respected, and secure in their abilities. By surrounding individuals with positive influences and role models who demonstrate confidence and resilience, they can learn to adopt similar attitudes and behaviors. Providing a safe space for individuals to express themselves, share their ideas, and take risks without fear of judgment or failure can help boost their confidence and self-esteem.

It is important to recognize that building self-confidence is a process that takes time and effort. It requires patience, persistence, and a willingness to confront and overcome self-doubt and insecurities. Encouraging self-compassion and self-care can help individuals develop a more positive and accepting attitude towards themselves. Practicing self-care activities such as mindfulness, meditation, exercise, and hobbies can help individuals reduce stress, increase self-awareness, and boost their confidence. By fostering a positive self-image, setting achievable goals, providing support and encouragement, and creating a supportive environment, individuals can build the self-confidence needed to navigate challenges, pursue their goals, and achieve success. Building self-confidence requires a combination of self-awareness, self-acceptance, and self-growth. It is an ongoing process that requires dedication, courage, and a belief in one's abilities. By implementing strategies to encourage self-confidence, individuals can unlock their full potential and experience a greater sense of fulfillment and achievement in various aspects of their lives.

- Positive Reinforcement

Positive reinforcement is a powerful tool in the field of psychology that has been shown to effectively modify behavior and encourage desired actions. It involves the presentation of a positive stimulus following a desired behavior, with the goal of increasing the likelihood that the behavior will occur again in the future. This approach is based on the principles of operant conditioning, which was developed by psychologist B. F. Skinner in the mid-20th century.

One key aspect of positive reinforcement is its emphasis on rewarding good behavior rather than punishing bad behavior. This is because research has shown that positive reinforcement is more effective in promoting lasting behavior change than punishment. When individuals are rewarded for their efforts or achievements, they are more likely to continue engaging in those behaviors in the future. In contrast, punishment may suppress unwanted behaviors temporarily, but it does not necessarily teach individuals what they should be doing instead.

Positive reinforcement can take many forms, from verbal praise and encouragement to tangible rewards such as stickers, tokens, or prizes. The key is to find something that is desirable and motivating for the individual receiving the reinforcement. It is important to tailor the reinforcement to the individual's preferences and needs in order for it to be effective. For example, a child who loves to read may be motivated by extra time to read their favorite book, while a teenager who enjoys video games may be motivated by earning time to play after completing their homework.

It is also important to consider the timing of the reinforcement. Ideally, the positive stimulus should be delivered immediately following the desired behavior in order to strengthen the association between the behavior and the reward. This is known as immediate reinforcement and has been shown to be more effective than delayed reinforcement. However, it is also possible to use delayed reinforcement, such as weekly allowances or quarterly bonuses, as long as there is a clear connection between the behavior and the reward.

In addition to timing, consistency is another important factor to consider when using positive reinforcement. In order for the reinforcement to be effective, it must be delivered consistently every time the desired behavior occurs. Inconsistency can weaken the association between the behavior and the reward, leading to diminished results. This is why it is crucial for caregivers, teachers, and other individuals implementing positive reinforcement strategies to be diligent and reliable in providing the reinforcement.

Another key aspect of positive reinforcement is shaping, which involves rewarding successive approximations of a desired behavior in order to gradually guide the individual towards the target behavior. This can be especially useful when working with complex behaviors that cannot be easily achieved all at once. By breaking down the behavior into smaller, more manageable steps and rewarding each step along the way, individuals can make progress towards their goals and build their skills and confidence over time. By rewarding individuals for their efforts and achievements, we can motivate them to continue engaging in positive behaviors and make lasting improvements in their lives. It is essential to understand the principles of positive reinforcement and apply them effectively in order to maximize their effectiveness. With careful planning, consistency, and tailored approaches, positive reinforcement can be a powerful tool for promoting positive behavior and helping individuals reach their full potential.

• • • •

- IMPORTANCE OF COLLABORATION

Collaboration is a fundamental aspect of human interaction and progress, both in personal and professional contexts. It involves individuals working together towards a common goal, pooling their resources, skills, and knowledge to achieve a shared objective. Collaboration is crucial in various fields, including business, academia, research, healthcare, and many others, as it allows individuals to leverage their unique strengths and expertise to solve complex problems, innovate, and drive meaningful change. In this essay, I will explore the importance of collaboration and its benefits, as well as provide practical tips for fostering effective collaboration in various settings.

One of the key advantages of collaboration is the diversity of perspectives and ideas it brings to the table. When individuals from different backgrounds, disciplines, and experiences come together to work on a project or solve a problem, they bring with them a wide range of viewpoints and insights. This diversity can lead to more creative and innovative solutions, as each team member can contribute their unique expertise and knowledge to the process. By collaborating with others, individuals can learn from one another, challenge their own assumptions, and gain new perspectives that can help them think more critically and creatively.

Collaboration also has the potential to increase efficiency and productivity. When individuals work together towards a common goal, they can divide the workload, leverage each other's strengths, and share resources to achieve their objectives more quickly and effectively. Collaboration can also help to streamline processes, eliminate duplication of effort, and promote better communication and coordination among team members. By working together, individuals can achieve more than they could on their own, leading to better outcomes and greater success in their endeavors.

Furthermore, collaboration can foster a sense of camaraderie and teamwork among individuals. When people collaborate effectively, they develop a sense of trust, mutual respect, and shared purpose that can enhance their working relationships and create a positive and supportive team environment. Collaboration can also lead to increased job satisfaction and engagement, as individuals feel valued, supported, and empowered to contribute their ideas and insights to the group. By fostering a culture of collaboration, organizations can create a more inclusive and harmonious work environment that values teamwork, diversity, and innovation.

In addition to these benefits, collaboration can also lead to personal and professional growth for individuals involved. By working with others, individuals can expand their skills, knowledge, and capabilities, as they learn from their colleagues, take on new challenges, and stretch themselves outside their comfort zones. Collaboration can also help individuals build their networks, establish new connections, and broaden their horizons as they engage with a diverse range of people and ideas. Moreover, collaborating with others can enhance an individual's problem-solving and decision-making skills, as they learn to navigate different perspectives, negotiate conflicting interests, and find common ground with their teammates.

Despite these numerous benefits, effective collaboration is not always easy to achieve. It requires clear communication, mutual respect, and trust among team members, as well as a shared commitment to the common goal and objectives. In order to foster collaboration in a group setting, individuals must be willing to listen to others, be open to new ideas and perspectives, and be willing to compromise and find common ground. Effective collaboration also requires strong leadership, clear roles and responsibilities, and a supportive team culture that values diversity, inclusivity, and innovation.

To foster effective collaboration in a professional or academic setting, there are several best practices and tips that individuals can follow. First and foremost, it is important to establish clear goals, objectives, and expectations for the collaboration, so that team members know what they are working towards and how their contributions will contribute to the overall success of the project. It is also essential to define roles and responsibilities, assign tasks and deadlines, and communicate effectively to ensure that everyone is on the same page and working towards a common purpose.

Furthermore, it is crucial to create a supportive and inclusive team environment that values diversity, respects different perspectives, and promotes open communication and collaboration. Team members should be encouraged to share their ideas and insights, ask questions, and seek feedback from others, in order to foster a culture of learning, growth, and innovation. It is also important to build trust and mutual respect among team members, through clear and honest communication, active listening, and a willingness to compromise and find common ground. Collaboration can bring diverse perspectives and ideas to the table, increase efficiency and productivity, foster teamwork and camaraderie, and lead to personal and professional growth for individuals involved. By following best practices and tips for fostering effective collaboration in various settings, individuals can maximize the benefits of collaboration and achieve greater success in their endeavors.

- Working Towards Common Goals

Working towards common goals is essential for any team or organization to be successful. When individuals collectively work towards a shared objective, they are able to pool their skills, knowledge, and resources to achieve greater outcomes than they could on their own. This collaborative approach fosters a sense of unity and cohesion among team members, as they are all committed to the same overarching goal. By aligning their efforts towards a common purpose, individuals can leverage each other's strengths and support one another in areas of weakness, leading to increased efficiency and productivity.

In order to effectively work towards common goals, it is crucial for team members to have a clear understanding of the objectives and priorities of the team or organization as a whole. This requires open and transparent communication among team members, as well as clear and concise goal setting by leadership. When everyone is on the same page and understands the direction in which they are heading, they can more easily align their individual efforts towards achieving the desired outcome. Regular check-ins and progress updates can help to keep everyone informed and motivated, ensuring that everyone remains focused on the common goal.

Collaboration is key when working towards common goals, as individuals must be willing to work together, share ideas, and support each other in order to be successful. This requires a high level of trust among team members, as well as the ability to communicate openly and honestly. It is important for individuals to be respectful of each other's perspectives and to be willing to compromise in order to reach a consensus. By fostering a collaborative and supportive environment, team members can leverage each other's strengths and work together to overcome challenges and obstacles that may arise during the goal-setting process.

Setting SMART goals can also be beneficial when working towards common objectives, as they provide a framework for defining specific, measurable, achievable, relevant, and time-bound targets. By setting goals that are clear and quantifiable, team members can more effectively track their progress and hold themselves accountable for achieving the desired outcomes. This can help to keep everyone focused and motivated, as they can see the tangible results of their efforts and celebrate their achievements along the way. SMART goals also provide a roadmap for success, outlining the steps that need to be taken in order to reach the desired outcome and helping to keep team members on track.

Effective leadership is essential when working towards common goals, as leaders play a crucial role in setting the direction and vision for the team or organization. Leaders must be able to effectively communicate the goals and priorities of the team, as well as inspire and motivate team members to work towards achieving them. They must also be able to provide direction, guidance, and support to team members, helping them to overcome challenges and navigate obstacles that may arise along the way. By leading by example and demonstrating a strong commitment to the common goal, leaders can inspire trust and confidence in their team members, encouraging them to give their best efforts and work together towards a shared objective. By aligning their efforts towards a shared objective, individuals can harness the power of collaboration and teamwork to achieve greater outcomes than they could on their own. Through open communication, collaboration, goal setting, and effective leadership, team members can work together to overcome challenges, leverage each other's strengths, and ultimately achieve success. By fostering a supportive and collaborative environment, team members can work towards common goals with confidence and enthusiasm, knowing that they are part of a unified effort to achieve a shared objective.

. . . .

- RESPECTING OTHERS' Differences

Respecting others' differences is an essential aspect of creating a harmonious and inclusive society. It involves accepting and valuing the unique qualities, beliefs, and perspectives that each person brings to the table. By acknowledging and celebrating diversity, we can promote understanding, empathy, and collaboration among individuals from different backgrounds. This not only enriches our personal relationships but also fosters a more supportive and welcoming community where everyone feels accepted and respected.

One important aspect of respecting others' differences is recognizing that diversity exists in various forms, including race, ethnicity, religion, gender, sexual orientation, age, ability, and socioeconomic status. Each person has a unique set of experiences, values, and cultural traditions that shape their identity and worldview. By being open-minded and curious about others' backgrounds, we can gain a better understanding of the complexities and nuances of different identities. This can help us challenge our own biases and prejudices, as well as promote a more inclusive and equitable society.

Furthermore, respecting others' differences involves actively listening to their perspectives and experiences without judgment or criticism. It requires us to approach conversations with empathy and openness, seeking to learn from others rather than impose our own beliefs or assumptions. By engaging in meaningful dialogue and creating a safe space for honest and respectful communication, we can build trust and mutual respect among individuals with diverse backgrounds. This can lead to deeper connections and a sense of community that transcends superficial differences.

In addition, respecting others' differences also means standing up against discrimination, prejudice, and injustice. It requires us to be allies and advocates for marginalized communities, speaking out against harmful stereotypes and discriminatory practices. By actively challenging systemic inequalities and working towards social justice, we can create a more equitable and inclusive society where everyone has the opportunity to thrive and be treated with dignity and respect. This involves supporting policies and initiatives that promote diversity, equity, and inclusion, as well as holding ourselves and others accountable for our actions and words. By embracing diversity and valuing the unique perspectives and experiences of others, we can create a more inclusive and supportive environment where everyone feels accepted and valued. It requires us to be open-minded, empathetic, and courageous in confronting prejudice and discrimination, as well as actively advocating for social justice and equity. Ultimately, by respecting others' differences, we can build a more vibrant, connected, and resilient society that celebrates the richness and complexity of human diversity.

- Setting Boundaries

Setting boundaries is a crucial aspect of maintaining healthy relationships, whether they be personal or professional. Boundaries are essentially guidelines that define what is acceptable and what is not in a given situation or relationship. They help to establish expectations, rights, and responsibilities for all parties involved. Setting boundaries can also help to protect your mental and emotional well-being by ensuring that you are not taken advantage of or treated unfairly.

In order to set effective boundaries, it is important to first understand what your own needs, values, and limits are. This self-awareness will enable you to clearly communicate your boundaries to others and enforce them when necessary. It is also important to recognize that boundaries are not set in stone and may need to be adjusted as circumstances change. Flexibility is key to maintaining healthy boundaries.

When setting boundaries, it is essential to communicate them clearly and assertively. This means expressing your needs and limits in a direct and respectful manner. It is important to avoid being passive or aggressive in your communication, as this can lead to misunderstandings or conflicts. Instead, assertiveness allows you to express yourself confidently while still considering the feelings and needs of others.

It is also important to remember that setting boundaries is not about controlling or punishing others. Instead, boundaries are about taking responsibility for your own well-being and ensuring that your needs are met. By setting boundaries, you are establishing a framework for healthy communication, respect, and reciprocity in your relationships.

In a professional setting, setting boundaries is equally important. It can help to define expectations and maintain a productive work environment. For example, setting boundaries around work hours, communication methods, and workload can help to prevent burnout and improve overall job satisfaction. Additionally, setting boundaries with clients, colleagues, and supervisors can help to establish clear roles and responsibilities, leading to more effective collaboration and communication. By understanding your own needs and values, communicating assertively, and being flexible when necessary, you can establish boundaries that promote respect, understanding, and mutual benefit in your personal and professional interactions. Remember that boundaries are not about control or punishment, but about creating a framework for healthy communication and mutual respect. By setting boundaries, you are taking responsibility for your own well-being and advocating for yourself in a positive and assertive manner.

Chapter 10: Encouraging Leadership Skills

• • • •

- EMPOWERING KIDS TO Take Initiative

Empowering children to take initiative is a crucial aspect of their development and growth. By instilling a sense of independence and autonomy in them, we are helping them to build essential skills that will serve them well throughout their lives. Encouraging kids to take initiative means giving them the confidence to make decisions and take action on their own, rather than always relying on adults to tell them what to do. This not only helps them to develop a sense of responsibility and self-reliance, but also fosters creativity, problem-solving abilities, and a willingness to try new things.

One of the key ways to empower kids to take initiative is to create a supportive and nurturing environment in which they feel safe to explore and take risks. This means providing them with opportunities to make choices and decisions, even if they may not always be the right ones. It is important for parents, teachers, and caregivers to encourage children to trust their own judgment and to learn from their mistakes. By giving kids the freedom to make decisions and take responsibility for their actions, we are helping them to develop a sense of agency and control over their own lives.

Another important aspect of empowering kids to take initiative is to provide them with the necessary tools and resources to succeed. This means offering them guidance, support, and encouragement as they navigate new challenges and experiences. It also means creating an environment that is conducive to learning and growth, where kids feel motivated and inspired to explore their interests and pursue their goals. By providing children with the resources they need to thrive, we are helping them to build confidence, resilience, and a sense of purpose that will serve them well in the future.

In addition to creating a supportive environment and providing the necessary tools and resources, it is also important to model initiative-taking behavior for kids to emulate. Children learn best by example, so it is essential for adults to demonstrate the importance of taking initiative in their own lives. This can be done by showing kids how to set goals, solve problems, and make decisions for themselves. By modeling initiative-taking behavior, we are helping kids to see that taking control of their own lives is not only possible, but also desirable. This can inspire them to take more risks, try new things, and pursue their passions with confidence and enthusiasm.

Ultimately, empowering kids to take initiative is about helping them to develop the skills and mindset they need to thrive in an ever-changing and complex world. By instilling a sense of independence, autonomy, and self-reliance in children, we are preparing them to navigate the challenges and opportunities that lie ahead with confidence and resilience. By creating a supportive environment, providing the necessary tools and resources, and modeling initiative-taking behavior, we can help kids to realize their full potential and become the confident, capable, and empowered individuals they are meant to be.

- Developing Decision-Making Skills

Decision-making is a crucial skill that everyone must possess in order to navigate through life's challenges and opportunities effectively. It is the process of identifying alternatives, evaluating them, and choosing the best course of action to achieve a desired outcome. Developing strong decision-making skills can lead to better outcomes in both personal and professional life, as well as improved confidence and problem-solving abilities.

There are several key components that contribute to effective decision-making. These include critical thinking, problem-solving, and emotional intelligence. Critical thinking is the ability to analyze and evaluate information objectively, without bias or preconceived notions. It involves asking questions, gathering evidence, and considering multiple perspectives before making a decision. Problem-solving is the process of identifying obstacles or challenges and developing strategies to overcome them. Emotional intelligence refers to the ability to understand and manage one's emotions, as well as to recognize and empathize with the emotions of others.

One important aspect of developing decision-making skills is gaining experience through practice. The more decisions we make, the more we learn about our own decision-making process and how to improve it. This can involve making small decisions on a daily basis, as well as tackling larger, more complex decisions when they arise. Seeking feedback from others can also be helpful in gaining insight into our decision-making abilities and identifying areas for improvement.

Another important aspect of developing decision-making skills is being able to manage uncertainty and risk. In many cases, decisions must be made with incomplete or uncertain information, and there is always a degree of risk involved. Being able to assess and manage this uncertainty and risk is crucial in making effective decisions. This may involve gathering more information, seeking advice from experts, or developing contingency plans in case things do not go as expected.

It is also important to consider the potential consequences of our decisions before making them. This involves thinking about how our decisions will impact ourselves and others, both in the short-term and long-term. Considering the ethical implications of our decisions is also important, as ethical considerations can often play a role in decision-making, particularly in professional settings.

In addition to these key components, there are several strategies that can help to improve decision-making skills. One such strategy is developing a decision-making process or framework to guide our decision-making. This may involve breaking down the decision into smaller steps, such as defining the problem, generating alternatives, evaluating the alternatives, making a decision, and implementing it. Having a structured process can help to ensure that all relevant factors are considered and that the decision is made in a systematic and logical way.

Another strategy is to avoid making decisions based on emotion or intuition alone. While emotions can provide valuable information about our preferences and values, they can also cloud our judgment and lead to biased decision-making. It is important to take a step back, consider the facts and evidence objectively, and make decisions based on logical reasoning rather than gut feelings.

Furthermore, seeking input from others can be a valuable strategy for improving decision-making skills. Consulting with colleagues, mentors, or experts in the field can provide valuable insights and perspectives that we may not have considered on our own. This can help to ensure that our decisions are well-informed and take into account a variety of viewpoints. By cultivating critical thinking, problem-solving, emotional intelligence, and other key components of effective decision-making, we can improve our ability to make sound decisions and achieve our goals. By incorporating strategies such as developing a decision-making process, managing uncertainty and risk, considering consequences, and seeking input from others, we can enhance our decision-making abilities and make better choices in all aspects of our lives.

Chapter 11: Cultivating Social Intelligence

. . . .

- READING SOCIAL SITUATIONS

Reading social situations is a crucial skill that helps individuals navigate the complexities of human interaction. It involves understanding the unspoken cues and signals that people send through their body language, tone of voice, and facial expressions. By being able to read these social cues, individuals can better assess the emotions, intentions, and attitudes of others, which enables them to respond appropriately in various social contexts.

One of the key aspects of reading social situations is being able to accurately interpret nonverbal communication. Nonverbal cues such as eye contact, gestures, posture, and facial expressions can provide valuable information about a person's emotional state and intentions. For example, a person who avoids eye contact and crosses their arms may be feeling defensive or closed off, while someone who maintains eye contact and smiles warmly may be feeling friendly and engaged. Paying attention to these nonverbal cues can help individuals gauge the mood of a social situation and adjust their behavior accordingly.

In addition to nonverbal cues, verbal communication also plays a crucial role in reading social situations. The tone of voice, pitch, volume, and pace of speech can all convey important emotional information that complements the words being spoken. For example, a sarcastic tone of voice can indicate that someone is not being serious, while a soft and soothing tone may suggest empathy or concern. By listening carefully to both the content and delivery of verbal communication, individuals can gain a more nuanced understanding of the underlying emotions and intentions of others.

Another important aspect of reading social situations is being attuned to the context in which interactions are taking place. Different social settings, such as a formal business meeting, a casual social gathering, or a family dinner, may have different expectations and norms for behavior. By being aware of the social context, individuals can adapt their communication style and behavior to fit the situation. For example, using formal language and maintaining professional boundaries may be more appropriate in a business setting, while using informal language and engaging in small talk may be more suitable in a social gathering.

One of the challenges of reading social situations is that individuals may not always be aware of the social cues they are sending or receiving. People's emotions and intentions are often complex and nuanced, and it can be easy to misinterpret or misunderstand the signals being communicated. In such cases, it is helpful to ask clarifying questions, seek feedback from others, or reflect on past experiences to gain a better understanding of the social dynamics at play. Developing self-awareness and empathy can also aid in improving one's ability to read social situations accurately. By paying attention to nonverbal and verbal cues, understanding the social context, and being aware of one's own biases and assumptions, individuals can enhance their ability to navigate social interactions effectively. Practicing active listening, asking questions, and seeking feedback can also help individuals refine their social skills and become more adept at reading social situations. Ultimately, being able to accurately interpret the thoughts and feelings of others can lead to better communication, stronger relationships, and more successful interactions in both personal and professional settings.

- Adapting to Different Social Contexts

Adapting to different social contexts is a crucial skill in today's interconnected world. As individuals navigate various social settings, such as work environments, social gatherings, and online platforms, they must be able to adjust their behavior, communication style, and even values to effectively interact and connect with others. This ability to adapt is not only important for building relationships and fostering collaboration but also for ensuring one's own personal growth and development.

One key aspect of adapting to different social contexts is understanding the cultural norms and expectations of a given setting. Different societies, communities, and even organizations may have their own unique customs, beliefs, and values that shape how individuals interact with one another. For example, in some cultures, direct and assertive communication may be preferred, while in others, indirect and subtle cues may be more appropriate. By being aware of and respectful of these cultural differences, individuals can avoid misunderstandings and conflicts and build stronger connections with others.

Another important factor in adapting to different social contexts is recognizing and adjusting to power dynamics. In many social settings, there are established hierarchies, whether explicit or implicit, that influence how individuals interact with one another. It is important for individuals to be mindful of these power dynamics and to adapt their behavior and communication style accordingly. For example, when interacting with a supervisor or authority figure, it may be necessary to show respect and deference, while in a more egalitarian setting, individuals may feel more comfortable speaking freely and openly.

Flexibility is also a key component of adapting to different social contexts. Being able to quickly assess a situation and adjust one's behavior and communication style can help individuals navigate unfamiliar or challenging social settings with ease. This ability to be flexible and adaptable can also help individuals build rapport with others and create positive impressions. By being open-minded and willing to try new approaches, individuals can demonstrate their ability to adapt and connect with others in a variety of social contexts.

In addition to cultural awareness, power dynamics, and flexibility, emotional intelligence is also an important skill for adapting to different social contexts. Emotional intelligence involves the ability to understand and manage one's own emotions as well as the emotions of others. By being empathetic and attuned to the feelings and moods of those around them, individuals can tailor their communication and behavior to better connect with others. This can lead to more meaningful and authentic interactions and help individuals build trust and mutual respect in different social settings. By honing these skills and actively seeking to understand and connect with others, individuals can navigate a variety of social settings with ease and confidence. This ability to adapt not only fosters positive relationships and collaboration but also promotes personal growth and development. In today's globalized and diverse world, the ability to adapt to different social contexts is a valuable skill that can lead to increased opportunities for success and fulfillment.

. . . .

- TEACHING KIDS ONLINE Etiquette

Teaching kids online etiquette is essential in today's digital age, as children are spending more and more time online for learning, entertainment, and communication. It is crucial for parents, educators, and caregivers to instill in children the importance of behaving respectfully and responsibly in the online world. Online etiquette, also known as netiquette, encompasses a variety of behaviors and practices that help maintain a positive and safe online environment. By teaching kids about online etiquette, we can help them navigate the digital landscape with confidence and integrity.

One of the key aspects of teaching kids online etiquette is emphasizing the importance of treating others with respect and kindness. Just as in face-to-face interactions, it is crucial for children to understand that their words and actions have an impact on others, even in the virtual realm. Teaching kids to think before they type and consider the feelings of others before posting or commenting online is a fundamental part of online etiquette. By promoting empathy and compassion in online interactions, we can help children develop into responsible and considerate digital citizens.

Another important aspect of teaching kids online etiquette is educating them about the potential risks and consequences of their online behavior. Children must understand that the internet is not a private space, and their actions online can have lasting implications. Teaching kids about online safety practices, such as protecting their personal information and being cautious about sharing photos or videos, is essential for their digital wellbeing. By setting clear expectations and boundaries around their online activities, parents and educators can help children make informed decisions and protect themselves from harm.

In addition to promoting respectful behavior and online safety, teaching kids about digital literacy is crucial for their success in the online world. Digital literacy encompasses the ability to critically evaluate information, communicate effectively, and navigate various online platforms and tools. By teaching kids how to verify the credibility of online sources, identify misinformation, and engage in respectful debates and discussions, we can empower them to make informed choices and contribute positively to online communities. Developing strong digital literacy skills will not only help children succeed academically but also prepare them for the complexities of the digital age.

Furthermore, teaching kids about the importance of digital citizenship is essential for fostering a sense of responsibility and accountability in their online interactions. Digital citizenship encompasses the rights, responsibilities, and ethics of using technology and digital media. By educating children about their rights and responsibilities as digital citizens, we can empower them to use technology ethically and responsibly. Teaching kids to respect intellectual property rights, practice good online behavior, and engage in meaningful and constructive online discussions is essential for promoting positive digital citizenship. By emphasizing the importance of respectful behavior, online safety, digital literacy, and digital citizenship, parents, educators, and caregivers can help children develop the skills and habits they need to thrive in the digital age. By instilling in children a strong foundation of online etiquette, we can empower them to make informed decisions, protect themselves from harm, and contribute positively to online communities. It is essential for adults to take an active role in teaching kids about online etiquette and modeling positive online behaviors themselves to create a safer and more positive digital landscape for future generations.

- Managing Screen Time

Managing screen time has become a crucial topic in today's digital age, where technology is deeply embedded in our daily lives. As screens have become integral to communication, education, work, and entertainment, it is important to establish healthy boundaries and practices to ensure that excessive screen time does not negatively impact our well-being. While screens serve as powerful tools, they also have the potential to cause health issues, such as eye strain, sleep disturbances, and mental health problems. Therefore, it is essential to prioritize managing screen time effectively to maintain a balanced and fulfilling lifestyle.

One of the key strategies in managing screen time is setting clear goals and boundaries for device usage. This involves establishing specific guidelines for how much time should be spent on screens each day, as well as designating "screen-free" times and spaces in your daily routine. By creating a structured plan for when and how screens can be used, individuals can prevent excessive and mindless scrolling, which often leads to time wasted and increased screen-related health issues. Setting boundaries can also help to promote healthier habits, such as physical activity, social interactions, and mindfulness practices, which are essential for overall well-being.

In addition to setting boundaries, it is important to be mindful of the quality of screen time activities. Not all screen time is created equal, and certain activities can have more negative effects on our health and well-being than others. For example, passive activities like watching endless hours of television or mindlessly scrolling through social media feeds can be detrimental to mental health and productivity. On the other hand, engaging in interactive and educational activities, such as online courses, creative projects, or meditation apps, can have positive effects on cognitive development and emotional well-being. Therefore, it is crucial to prioritize high-quality screen time activities that enrich our lives rather than deplete our energy.

Another important aspect of managing screen time is understanding the impact of screens on our physical and mental health. Excessive screen time has been linked to a myriad of health issues, including eye strain, headaches, neck and back pain, sleep disturbances, and decreased social interactions. The blue light emitted from screens can disrupt our circadian rhythms and affect the quality of our sleep, leading to fatigue and cognitive impairment. Moreover, prolonged screen use can also contribute to sedentary behavior and physical health problems, such as obesity and cardiovascular diseases. By being aware of the potential negative effects of screen time, individuals can take proactive steps to mitigate these risks and prioritize their well-being.

One effective strategy for managing screen time is to practice mindfulness and intentional screen use. Mindfulness involves being present and engaged in the moment, rather than mindlessly scrolling through screens or multitasking with multiple devices. By cultivating mindfulness in our screen time activities, we can enhance our focus, attention, and productivity, while also reducing stress and anxiety. Intentional screen use, on the other hand, involves purposefully choosing how and when to use screens based on our goals and values. This might include setting specific intentions for screen time, such as learning new skills, connecting with loved ones, or engaging in creative projects, rather than simply using screens out of habit or boredom.

Moreover, it is important to prioritize digital well-being practices that promote a healthy relationship with screens. This includes taking regular breaks from screens, practicing good posture and ergonomics, and maintaining a balanced lifestyle that includes physical activity, social interactions, and self-care activities. By incorporating these practices into our daily routines, we can prevent screen-related health issues and foster a more mindful and intentional approach to using technology. Additionally, seeking support from friends, family, or mental health professionals can be beneficial in managing screen time and addressing any underlying issues that may be contributing to excessive screen use. By setting clear boundaries, prioritizing high-quality screen time activities, understanding the impact of screens on our health, practicing mindfulness and intentional screen use, and prioritizing digital well-being practices, individuals can cultivate a healthy relationship with screens and harness the benefits of technology while minimizing the risks. By taking proactive steps to manage screen time effectively, we can enhance our well-being, improve our productivity, and cultivate a more mindful and intentional approach to using technology in our daily lives.

Chapter 13: Encouraging Inclusivity

••••

- CELEBRATING DIVERSITY

Diversity is a concept that is increasingly becoming recognized as a key element in the success of organizations, communities, and societies as a whole. Celebrating diversity involves acknowledging and embracing the different backgrounds, experiences, and perspectives that individuals bring to the table. It is about creating an environment where all individuals are valued and respected for who they are, regardless of their race, ethnicity, gender, sexual orientation, religion, or any other characteristic. By celebrating diversity, organizations can harness the unique strengths and talents of each individual, leading to increased innovation, creativity, and overall success.

One of the key benefits of celebrating diversity is the ability to create a more inclusive and welcoming environment for all individuals. When people feel accepted and valued for who they are, they are more likely to feel motivated and engaged in their work or community activities. This leads to higher levels of job satisfaction, increased productivity, and overall well-being. By promoting diversity and inclusion, organizations can attract and retain top talent from a wide range of backgrounds, perspectives, and experiences. This not only brings a greater diversity of thought and ideas to the table but also helps to create a more dynamic and high-performing team.

Another important aspect of celebrating diversity is the opportunity it provides for learning and growth. When individuals from different backgrounds come together, they have the chance to learn from one another, challenge their own assumptions, and broaden their perspectives. This can lead to greater empathy, understanding, and appreciation for the diverse experiences of others. By fostering an environment of diversity and inclusion, organizations can promote a culture of continuous learning and professional development, which is essential for staying competitive in today's fast-paced and ever-changing world. Additionally, celebrating diversity can help to break down barriers and address issues of discrimination and inequality, creating a more just and equitable society for all.

In addition to the many benefits for organizations and communities, celebrating diversity also has personal and societal benefits. When individuals feel accepted and valued for who they are, they are more likely to feel a sense of belonging and connection to others. This can lead to greater levels of happiness, fulfillment, and overall well-being. By celebrating diversity, we can create a more vibrant and inclusive society where all individuals can thrive and reach their full potential. Embracing diversity also helps to build stronger relationships and connections across different groups, leading to greater social cohesion and harmony.

It is important to recognize that celebrating diversity is not just a one-time event or initiative, but rather a continuous and ongoing process. In order to truly embrace diversity and create a more inclusive environment, organizations and communities must be committed to promoting diversity and inclusion in all aspects of their operations. This includes fostering a culture of respect and acceptance, implementing policies and practices that promote diversity, and providing opportunities for individuals from different backgrounds to collaborate and learn from one another. By making diversity a priority and actively promoting an inclusive environment, organizations can create a more welcoming and supportive space for all individuals to thrive and succeed. By embracing and valuing the unique contributions of individuals from all backgrounds, we can harness the power of diversity to drive innovation, growth, and success. By fostering a culture of respect, acceptance, and inclusion, organizations can attract and retain top talent, promote learning and growth, and create a more just and equitable society for all. Ultimately, celebrating diversity is not just the right thing to do – it is essential for creating a more vibrant, inclusive, and successful world for everyone.

- Creating a Welcoming Environment

Creating a welcoming environment is a crucial aspect of promoting inclusivity and fostering a sense of belonging within any organization or community. A welcoming environment is one where individuals feel accepted, respected, and valued for who they are, regardless of their background, beliefs, or identity. It is a space where everyone feels safe to express themselves, share their ideas, and collaborate with others without fear of discrimination or prejudice.

Building a welcoming environment requires intentional effort and a commitment to creating a culture of diversity, equity, and inclusion.

One of the key elements of creating a welcoming environment is promoting open communication and dialogue among members of the community. Open communication allows individuals to express their thoughts and feelings freely, share their perspectives, and engage in meaningful conversations with others. This fosters a sense of connection and understanding among community members, leading to stronger relationships and a more cohesive environment. By encouraging open communication, we can create a culture of respect and inclusivity where everyone's voice is heard and valued.

Another important aspect of creating a welcoming environment is promoting diversity and celebrating differences among community members. Diversity is a strength that brings a variety of perspectives, experiences, and ideas to the table, which can lead to innovation, creativity, and growth. By embracing diversity and recognizing the unique contributions of each individual, we can create a culture that values inclusivity and promotes equality. Celebrating differences can help break down barriers, challenge biases, and create a more welcoming and inclusive environment for everyone.

In addition to promoting open communication and embracing diversity, creating a welcoming environment also requires establishing clear policies and guidelines to ensure that all members of the community are treated with respect and dignity. This includes implementing anti-discrimination policies, providing resources and support for individuals facing discrimination or harassment, and holding members accountable for their actions. By setting clear expectations and consequences for inappropriate behavior, we can create a safe and inclusive environment where everyone feels welcome and valued.

Furthermore, creating a welcoming environment involves providing opportunities for community members to engage with each other, build relationships, and collaborate on projects and initiatives. This can be done through social events, networking opportunities, mentorship programs, and other activities that encourage interaction and collaboration among members. By creating opportunities for community members to connect and work together, we can strengthen relationships, build trust, and foster a sense of belonging that contributes to a more welcoming and inclusive environment.

Ultimately, creating a welcoming environment is about creating a culture of respect, inclusivity, and equity where everyone feels accepted and valued for who they are. It requires intentional effort, commitment, and collaboration among community members to build a space that is safe, supportive, and welcoming for all. By promoting open communication, embracing diversity, establishing clear policies, and providing opportunities for engagement, we can create an environment that fosters connection, understanding, and collaboration among all members of the community. Through these efforts, we can create a welcoming environment that promotes inclusivity, strengthens relationships, and enhances the overall well-being of our community.

• • • •

- MANNERS AND POLITENESS

Manners and politeness play a crucial role in the way we interact with others in various social settings. These concepts encompass a wide range of behaviors and practices that help us navigate social situations with grace and consideration for others. While manners may vary across cultures and contexts, the underlying principles of respect, courtesy, and consideration for others are universal.

In today's fast-paced and technology-driven world, the importance of manners and politeness may sometimes be overlooked or dismissed as old-fashioned. However, these timeless values continue to be essential for building strong relationships, fostering teamwork, and creating a positive work or social environment. When individuals exhibit good manners and politeness, they demonstrate respect for themselves and others, which can lead to greater trust, cooperation, and mutual understanding.

One of the key components of good manners is consideration for others. This involves being mindful of how our words and actions affect those around us and making an effort to treat others with kindness and empathy. Simple gestures such as saying "please" and "thank you," holding the door open for someone, or offering a sincere compliment can go a long way in creating a positive impression and fostering goodwill. By showing consideration for others, we create a more inclusive and harmonious social environment where everyone feels valued and respected.

Politeness is another important aspect of social interaction that is closely related to manners. Politeness involves using language and behavior that is considerate, respectful, and appropriate for a given situation. This includes using polite phrases and gestures, avoiding offensive or disrespectful language, and being attentive to social cues and norms. Politeness helps to establish a sense of mutual respect and courtesy in our interactions with others, creating a more pleasant and harmonious social environment.

In professional settings, good manners and politeness are particularly important for building rapport, establishing credibility, and fostering positive relationships with colleagues, clients, and customers. By demonstrating respect, courtesy, and consideration for others, we create a professional image that reflects well on ourselves and our organization. In a competitive business environment, individuals who practice good manners and politeness are more likely to be perceived as trustworthy, reliable, and professional, which can lead to greater success and opportunities for career advancement.

While the rules of etiquette and social conventions may evolve over time, the underlying principles of manners and politeness remain constant. These values serve as a foundation for creating a more civil, respectful, and harmonious society where individuals can interact with one another in a positive and constructive manner. By cultivating good manners and politeness in our daily interactions, we can contribute to a more inclusive and empathetic social environment that values diversity, kindness, and respect for others. By practicing good manners and politeness in our daily interactions, we demonstrate respect, courtesy, and consideration for others, which can lead to greater trust, cooperation, and mutual understanding. In professional settings, good manners and politeness are particularly important for establishing credibility, building rapport, and fostering positive relationships with colleagues, clients, and customers. Ultimately, by embracing the principles of manners and politeness, we can contribute to a more civil, respectful, and inclusive society where individuals can interact with one another in a positive and constructive manner.

- Making Introductions

Making introductions is a common social practice that helps establish connections and build relationships between people in various contexts. Whether it be in a professional setting, a social event, or a casual gathering, knowing how to properly introduce individuals can set a positive tone and facilitate communication. By following some basic etiquette guidelines and being mindful of cultural differences, anyone can master the art of making introductions and make a positive impression on others.

One of the key factors to keep in mind when making introductions is to always start with the person of higher status or authority. This shows respect and acknowledges their position in the conversation or setting. For example, if you are introducing your boss to a new employee, it is important to say, "Mr. Smith, I would like you to meet our new employee, Jane. " By giving precedence to the person of higher status, you are demonstrating proper deference and establishing a sense of hierarchy within the interaction.

In addition to acknowledging hierarchical differences, it is also important to be mindful of cultural norms and customs when making introductions. Different cultures may have varying expectations and protocols for introducing individuals, so it is important to be aware of these differences and adjust your approach accordingly. For example, in some cultures, it may be considered disrespectful to address someone by their first name without their explicit permission, while in others, using titles and honorifics may be the norm. By being mindful of cultural nuances, you can avoid inadvertent misunderstandings and ensure that your introductions are well-received.

Another key aspect of making introductions is to provide some context or background information about the individuals being introduced. This can help facilitate conversation and establish common ground between the parties. For example, if you are introducing two colleagues who work in the same department but have never met, you could say something like, "John, this is Susan. She also works in our marketing department and recently completed a successful campaign for a new product launch. " By providing some context about the individuals being introduced, you are giving them an opportunity to find common interests or topics of conversation, which can help break the ice and facilitate a more meaningful interaction.

Furthermore, it is important to be clear and concise when making introductions. Stick to the essential information, such as the names of the individuals and any relevant context, and avoid veering off into unrelated tangents. By keeping your introductions simple and to the point, you can ensure that the focus remains on the individuals being introduced and their interaction. In these instances, it is perfectly acceptable to ask for guidance or clarification from someone more experienced or knowledgeable about the context. For example, if you are attending a formal event and are unsure of how to introduce a guest to the host, you could discreetly ask a staff member or another guest for help. By seeking assistance when needed, you can demonstrate humility and a willingness to learn, which can enhance your social skills and make you more adept at making introductions in the future. By following etiquette guidelines, being mindful of cultural differences, providing context, and being clear and concise, anyone can master the art of making introductions and make a positive impression on others. Remember to always start with the person of higher status, be aware of cultural norms, provide relevant information, and seek guidance when needed. With practice and attention to detail, you can become a proficient introducer and enhance your interpersonal skills in any situation.

49

. . . .

- COPING STRATEGIES for Managing Emotions

Emotions are an essential aspect of human experience, influencing our thoughts, behaviors, and overall well-being. While emotions can be positive and bring joy, they can also be overwhelming and challenging to manage. Coping strategies play a crucial role in helping individuals navigate their emotions effectively and maintain mental health. In this discussion, we will explore various coping strategies for managing emotions and delve into their benefits and practical applications.

One of the most effective coping strategies for managing emotions is mindfulness. Mindfulness involves being aware of the present moment without judgment and accepting one's thoughts and feelings. By practicing mindfulness, individuals can develop a greater sense of self-awareness and emotional regulation. Research has shown that mindfulness can reduce stress, anxiety, and depression by promoting relaxation and enhancing cognitive flexibility. Mindfulness practices, such as meditation, deep breathing, and body scans, can help individuals become more attuned to their emotions and respond to them in a balanced and constructive manner.

Another valuable coping strategy for managing emotions is cognitive restructuring. Cognitive restructuring involves identifying and challenging negative thought patterns that contribute to emotional distress. By replacing negative thoughts with more positive and rational ones, individuals can change their emotional responses and improve their overall well-being. Cognitive restructuring techniques include reframing negative beliefs, practicing gratitude, and cultivating self-compassion. By incorporating cognitive restructuring into their daily routine, individuals can develop a more resilient mindset and navigate challenging emotions with greater ease.

In addition to mindfulness and cognitive restructuring, social support is a crucial coping strategy for managing emotions. Social support involves seeking help and comfort from friends, family, or other trusted individuals during times of emotional difficulty. By sharing their feelings and experiences with others, individuals can gain perspective, validation, and emotional connection. Research has shown that social support can reduce feelings of loneliness, isolation, and despair, and enhance overall emotional well-being. Building a strong support network and maintaining healthy relationships can provide individuals with a sense of security and belonging, empowering them to cope with their emotions more effectively.

Physical exercise is another powerful coping strategy for managing emotions. Regular physical activity can enhance mood, reduce stress, and improve overall mental health. Exercise releases endorphins, the body's natural feel-good chemicals, which can boost mood and reduce feelings of anxiety and depression. Engaging in physical exercise, such as walking, jogging, yoga, or dancing, can help individuals release pent-up emotions, increase energy levels, and improve sleep quality. By incorporating regular exercise into their routine, individuals can build resilience against emotional challenges and cultivate a healthier mind-body connection.

Furthermore, creative expression is a valuable coping strategy for managing emotions. Engaging in creative activities, such as art, music, writing, or dance, can provide individuals with a means of self-expression and emotional release. Creative expression allows individuals to channel their emotions into a tangible form, helping them process and make sense of their feelings. Research has shown that creative expression can reduce stress, enhance self-awareness, and promote emotional healing. By finding a creative outlet that resonates with them, individuals can explore their emotions, gain insight into their inner world, and nurture their emotional well-being. By incorporating mindfulness, cognitive restructuring, social support, physical exercise, and creative expression into their daily routine, individuals can develop resilience, emotional intelligence, and a sense of well-being. While coping with difficult emotions can be challenging, it is important to remember that seeking support and utilizing healthy coping strategies can help individuals navigate their emotions with grace and fortitude. By prioritizing self-care, emotional regulation, and positive coping mechanisms, individuals can cultivate a strong foundation for managing their emotions and leading a fulfilling life.

- Handling Stressful Situations

Handling stressful situations is an essential skill that everyone must learn in order to navigate the challenges of life effectively. Stress is a natural reaction to difficult or threatening circumstances, and it can manifest in a variety of ways, such as physical symptoms like headaches or stomachaches, emotional symptoms like anxiety or irritability, or behavioral symptoms like difficulty concentrating or increased use of substances like alcohol or drugs. While stress is a normal part of life, chronic or overwhelming stress can have serious negative impacts on both our physical and mental health.

One of the first steps in handling stressful situations is to recognize the signs of stress in ourselves. By being aware of the physical, emotional, and behavioral symptoms of stress, we can take proactive steps to address our stress before it becomes overwhelming. This might involve taking a moment to check in with ourselves and assess how we are feeling, or it might involve seeking input from others who can help us recognize when we are becoming stressed.

Once we have recognized that we are experiencing stress, the next step is to identify the source of that stress. This might seem obvious, but it can be surprisingly difficult to pinpoint the specific cause of our stress. Sometimes stress comes from external sources, like a demanding job or a challenging relationship, while other times it stems from internal sources, like our own negative self-talk or unrealistic expectations of ourselves. By identifying the source of our stress, we can take steps to address it in a more targeted and effective way.

After identifying the source of our stress, the next step is to develop a plan for managing that stress. This might involve setting boundaries with others, practicing relaxation techniques like deep breathing or meditation, seeking support from friends or family members, or making changes to our environment or lifestyle. It's important to remember that everyone is different, so what works for one person may not work for another. It might take some trial and error to find the strategies that work best for us, but with persistence and patience, we can learn to manage our stress in a healthy and effective way.

In addition to developing a plan for managing our stress, it's also important to take care of ourselves physically. This might involve getting regular exercise, eating a healthy diet, getting enough sleep, and avoiding substances like caffeine, alcohol, and drugs that can exacerbate our stress. Physical self-care can have a powerful impact on our mental and emotional well-being, so it's important to prioritize taking care of our bodies as a way of managing our stress.

Another important aspect of handling stressful situations is practicing self-compassion. It's easy to be hard on ourselves when we are stressed, blaming ourselves for not handling the situation better or feeling guilty for feeling stressed in the first place. But self-compassion involves treating ourselves with the same kindness, understanding, and support that we would offer to a friend in a similar situation. By practicing self-compassion, we can develop a more positive and nurturing relationship with ourselves, which can help us cope with stress more effectively.

In addition to self-compassion, seeking support from others can also be incredibly helpful in handling stressful situations. Talking to friends, family members, or a therapist about our stress can provide us with a new perspective on our situation, help us feel less alone, and offer practical advice and support. It's important to remember that asking for help is a sign of strength, not weakness, and that reaching out to others for support is a healthy and effective way of coping with stress.

To bring to a close, it's important to remember that stress is a normal part of life and that it's okay to feel stressed from time to time. By learning to recognize the signs of stress, identifying the sources of our stress, developing a plan for managing our stress, taking care of ourselves physically, practicing self-compassion, and seeking support from others, we can learn to handle stressful situations in a healthy and effective way. With practice and persistence, we can develop the resilience and coping skills needed to navigate life's challenges with grace and confidence.

. . . .

- RECOGNIZING BULLYING Behaviors

Bullying is a pervasive issue that can have serious consequences for those who experience it. Recognizing bullying behaviors is an important step in addressing and preventing this harmful behavior. Bullying can take on many forms, including physical, verbal, and cyberbullying. Physical bullying involves physically harming or intimidating someone, while verbal bullying includes name-calling, teasing, and spreading rumors. Cyberbullying occurs online, through social media or text messages, and can be just as harmful as traditional forms of bullying.

One key aspect of recognizing bullying behaviors is understanding the power dynamics at play. Bullying often involves a power imbalance, with the bully exerting control over the victim. This can manifest in a variety of ways, such as age, size, popularity, or social status. By recognizing these power dynamics, we can better understand the underlying causes of bullying behavior and work towards addressing them.

Another important aspect of recognizing bullying behaviors is being able to distinguish between conflict and bullying. Conflict is a normal part of human interaction and can involve disagreements or arguments between individuals. However, bullying is different in that it is intentional, repetitive, and involves a power imbalance. By understanding the distinction between conflict and bullying, we can better address and prevent harmful behaviors.

It is also important to recognize the warning signs of bullying behaviors. These can include changes in behavior, such as withdrawal, anxiety, or depression, as well as physical symptoms like headaches or stomachaches. Victims of bullying may also exhibit changes in academic performance or a reluctance to attend school. By being aware of these warning signs, we can intervene early and provide support to those who are experiencing bullying.

In addition to recognizing the warning signs of bullying, it is important to be aware of the different roles that individuals can play in a bullying situation. In addition to the bully and the victim, there are also bystanders who witness the bullying behavior. Bystanders may either assist the bully, support the victim, or remain passive and do nothing. By understanding the role of bystanders in bullying situations, we can empower them to take action and intervene when they see harmful behavior.

When addressing and preventing bullying behaviors, it is important to create a safe and inclusive environment where individuals feel comfortable reporting incidents of bullying. This can involve implementing clear policies and procedures for addressing bullying, as well as providing education and training on bullying prevention. By fostering a culture of respect and empathy, we can create a community where bullying behaviors are not tolerated and all individuals feel safe and supported. By understanding the power dynamics at play, distinguishing between conflict and bullying, recognizing warning signs, and addressing the different roles that individuals can play in a bullying situation, we can create a safe and inclusive environment where bullying is not tolerated. Through education, training, and proactive intervention, we can work towards creating a community where all individuals feel respected, supported, and empowered.

- Empowering Kids to Stand Up to Bullying

Bullying is a pervasive issue that can have lasting negative impacts on children's mental and emotional well-being. Research has shown that children who are bullied are more likely to experience anxiety, depression, and low self-esteem. In order to combat this issue, it is important for children to feel empowered to stand up to bullying and advocate for themselves and others.

Empowering kids to stand up to bullying involves teaching them important skills such as self-confidence, assertiveness, and empathy. By helping children develop these skills, they are better equipped to handle situations where they may encounter bullying behavior. Teaching children to stand up for themselves and others not only helps to prevent bullying, but also fosters a sense of community and support among peers.

One way to empower kids to stand up to bullying is through education and awareness. Schools and parents can work together to educate children about what constitutes bullying behavior and how to effectively respond to it. By teaching children about the different forms of bullying, such as verbal, physical, and cyberbullying, they are better able to recognize when they or others are being bullied.

Another important aspect of empowering kids to stand up to bullying is fostering a supportive and inclusive school culture. Schools can implement bullying prevention programs that promote positive behavior and teach students how to support their peers. By creating a supportive environment where students feel comfortable speaking up about bullying, schools can empower children to stand up for themselves and others.

In addition to education and awareness, it is important for parents and educators to model positive behavior and communication skills for children. By demonstrating empathy, respect, and assertiveness in their own interactions, adults can serve as role models for children on how to effectively respond to bullying behavior. Encouraging open communication and support networks both at home and in school can help children feel empowered to address bullying situations.

Empowering kids to stand up to bullying is not just about teaching them how to respond in the moment, but also about building their resilience and self-esteem. By helping children build their confidence and self-worth, they are better able to navigate challenging situations and advocate for themselves. Encouraging children to practice self-care and engage in activities that promote their well-being can help them develop the resilience needed to stand up to bullying. By teaching children important skills, fostering a supportive school culture, and modeling positive behavior, parents and educators can help empower children to advocate for themselves and others. Through education, awareness, and support, we can work together to combat bullying and create a more inclusive and respectful community for all children.

• • • •

- ENGAGING IN COMMUNITY Service

Engaging in community service is a valuable and rewarding experience that allows individuals to give back to their communities and make a positive impact on the world around them. Community service involves volunteering time and resources to help others in need, whether it be through organized events, non-profit organizations, or individual acts of kindness. By participating in community service, individuals have the opportunity to strengthen their sense of social responsibility, develop new skills, and build meaningful relationships with others in their community.

One of the key benefits of engaging in community service is the opportunity to contribute to the well-being of others and make a positive difference in the world. By volunteering time and resources to help those in need, individuals can provide support and assistance to marginalized populations, improve the quality of life for those facing adversity, and help build stronger, more resilient communities. Community service allows individuals to address social issues and contribute to positive social change, giving them a sense of purpose and fulfillment in their lives.

In addition to the social impact of community service, engaging in volunteer work can also have personal benefits for individuals. By participating in community service, individuals have the opportunity to develop new skills, gain hands-on experience, and learn more about themselves and the world around them. Through volunteer work, individuals can strengthen their communication, problem-solving, and leadership skills, as well as develop a greater sense of empathy, compassion, and understanding for others. By engaging in community service, individuals can broaden their horizons, expand their knowledge and perspective, and grow as individuals.

Another important aspect of community service is the opportunity to build meaningful relationships with others in the community. By volunteering time and resources to help others, individuals have the opportunity to connect with like-minded people, build friendships, and create a sense of community and belonging. Community service provides individuals with the opportunity to work together towards a common goal, share experiences and stories, and support each other in times of need. By engaging in community service, individuals can forge lasting bonds with others in their community, creating a sense of unity and solidarity that can enrich their lives and the lives of those around them.

Engaging in community service can take many different forms, from participating in organized events and programs to volunteering with non-profit organizations or simply performing acts of kindness for those in need. There are numerous ways for individuals to get involved in community service, whether it be through local charities, schools, churches, or community centers. By exploring different opportunities for volunteer work, individuals can find a cause or a program that resonates with them and aligns with their values and interests. Whether it's working with children, the elderly, the homeless, or the environment, there are countless ways for individuals to contribute to the well-being of their communities and make a positive impact on the world around them. By volunteering time and resources to help those in need, individuals can contribute to positive social change, develop new skills, and grow as individuals. Whether it's participating in organized events, volunteering with non-profit organizations, or simply performing acts of kindness for those in need, there are countless ways for individuals to get involved in community service and make a difference in the world. So, let's come together, lend a helping hand, and make our communities a better place for all.

- Teaching the Importance of Giving Back

Teaching the importance of giving back is an essential aspect of education that fosters empathy, compassion, and social responsibility in individuals. By instilling the value of generosity and philanthropy in students, educators can help shape a more equitable and caring society. Giving back not only benefits the recipients of charitable acts but also promotes personal growth, mental well-being, and a sense of purpose in the givers themselves. In this essay, we will explore the various ways in which educators can teach the importance of giving back to their students, as well as the positive impacts that volunteering and philanthropy can have on individuals and communities.

One of the most effective ways to teach the importance of giving back is through role modeling. Educators can set an example for their students by engaging in acts of service and charitable giving themselves. By demonstrating generosity and compassion in their own actions, teachers can inspire students to follow suit and make a positive difference in their communities. Additionally, educators can invite guest speakers or community leaders to share their experiences with philanthropy and volunteerism, providing real-life examples of the impact that giving back can have.

Another important aspect of teaching the importance of giving back is incorporating service-learning projects into the curriculum. Service-learning allows students to apply classroom knowledge to real-world situations while addressing community needs. By engaging in service projects, students can develop empathy, leadership skills, and a sense of civic duty. These experiences not only benefit the recipients of the service but also help students to develop a greater understanding of social issues and inspire them to continue giving back throughout their lives.

Moreover, educators can use storytelling and literature to teach the importance of giving back. By reading and discussing stories of generosity, kindness, and selflessness, students can learn about the impact that acts of service can have on individuals and communities. Literature can also help students to develop empathy and perspective-taking skills, enabling them to understand the needs of others and the importance of giving back to those less fortunate. Through discussions and reflections on literature, educators can encourage students to think critically about the role of charity and volunteerism in society.

In addition to role modeling, service-learning, and literature, educators can also incorporate discussions about social justice and equity into their teaching of giving back. By exploring the root causes of social issues such as poverty, inequality, and discrimination, students can develop a deeper understanding of the systemic barriers that prevent individuals from thriving. Educators can facilitate conversations about privilege, power dynamics, and the importance of advocating for social change. By equipping students with the knowledge and tools to address social injustices, educators can inspire them to take action and make a positive impact in their communities.

Furthermore, educators can teach the importance of giving back by integrating lessons on financial literacy and responsible stewardship into their curriculum. By helping students understand the value of money, budgeting, and saving, educators can empower them to make informed decisions about charitable giving and philanthropy. By teaching students to be thoughtful and intentional about their financial donations, educators can help them maximize the impact of their generosity and ensure that their contributions are directed towards causes that align with their values and beliefs. Additionally, educators can educate students about the importance of supporting local businesses, non-profit organizations, and social enterprises that are working to address pressing social issues in their communities. By incorporating role modeling, service-learning, literature, social justice discussions, and financial literacy lessons into their teaching, educators can inspire students to make a positive difference in their communities and advocate for social change. Through these strategies, educators can help shape a more equitable and caring society where giving back is not only valued but celebrated as a fundamental aspect of being a responsible and compassionate member of society.

Chapter 18: Supporting Social Skill Development in Children with Special Needs

. . . .

- STRATEGIES FOR INCLUSIVE Education

Inclusive education is a philosophy that goes beyond simply placing students with disabilities in mainstream classrooms. It is a commitment to providing all students, regardless of their background, abilities, or learning styles, with the support and resources they need to thrive in an educational setting. Inclusive education is about creating a welcoming and supportive environment where all students feel valued and included, and where every student has the opportunity to reach their full potential.

There are several key strategies that can be implemented to promote inclusive education in schools. One of the most important strategies is to create a school culture that values diversity and inclusivity. This means actively promoting respect, empathy, and understanding among students, teachers, and staff. It also means fostering a sense of belonging and acceptance for all students, regardless of their differences.

Another important strategy for promoting inclusive education is to provide appropriate support and accommodations for students with disabilities or other learning needs. This may include providing additional resources, such as assistive technology or specialized instruction, as well as modifying curriculum and instructional methods to meet the needs of diverse learners. It is crucial that schools have systems in place to identify students who may require additional support, and to ensure that those students receive the necessary accommodations and services to succeed.

Inclusive education also involves collaborating with families, community organizations, and other stakeholders to support students' learning and development. When schools work together with parents and caregivers, they can create a more holistic approach to education that considers the whole child and all aspects of their well-being. By involving families and communities in the educational process, schools can build stronger relationships with students and their support networks, and can better address the unique needs and challenges that students may face.

Inclusive education is not just about meeting the needs of students with disabilities; it is about recognizing and celebrating the diversity of all students. This means providing opportunities for students to learn about and appreciate different cultures, languages, and perspectives, and to develop empathy and understanding for others. Schools can promote inclusivity by incorporating diverse perspectives into the curriculum, creating a welcoming and inclusive physical environment, and organizing events and activities that celebrate diversity and promote inclusivity.

Inclusive education is a complex and multifaceted endeavor that requires ongoing commitment and collaboration from all members of the school community. It is not simply a set of policies or practices, but a fundamental shift in how we think about education and how we support the learning and development of all students. By implementing strategies that promote inclusivity, respect, and support for all students, schools can create a more welcoming and supportive environment where every student can thrive.

- Building Supportive Networks

Building supportive networks is crucial for personal and professional development. These networks provide a sense of belonging, help in times of need, and offer valuable resources and connections. Supportive networks can consist of friends, family, colleagues, mentors, and other individuals who provide encouragement, guidance, and assistance as needed. Building and maintaining these networks requires effort and commitment but can lead to increased satisfaction, success, and well-being in both personal and professional life.

One of the key benefits of having a supportive network is the emotional support it provides. In today's fast-paced and often isolating world, having a group of individuals who are there to listen, offer advice, and provide encouragement is invaluable. Whether facing personal challenges, setbacks at work, or difficult decisions, having a supportive network can help individuals navigate through these experiences with more resilience and confidence. Research has shown that having a strong support system can lead to better mental health outcomes, lower levels of stress, and increased overall well-being.

In addition to emotional support, supportive networks can also offer practical assistance and resources. For example, a supportive colleague may be able to provide helpful feedback on a work project, a mentor may offer guidance on career advancement, or a friend may connect you with a valuable contact in your industry. By tapping into the resources and expertise of your network, you can gain new insights, opportunities, and skills that can help you grow and succeed in your personal and professional life.

Building a supportive network requires effort and intentionality. It is important to actively cultivate relationships with individuals who share your values, interests, and goals. This may involve attending networking events, joining professional organizations, or simply reaching out to old friends and colleagues to reconnect. Building a diverse network of individuals from different backgrounds and industries can also be beneficial, as it can provide you with a wider range of perspectives and opportunities for growth and learning.

Maintaining supportive networks also requires ongoing effort and communication. It is important to stay in touch with your network, check in on their well-being, and offer support and assistance whenever possible. By being a reliable and supportive member of your network, you can strengthen your relationships and build a sense of reciprocity and trust that can be beneficial for all involved. These networks can provide emotional support, practical assistance, and valuable resources that can help individuals navigate through challenges, achieve their goals, and lead more fulfilling lives. By investing in your relationships and actively cultivating a diverse and supportive network, you can create a strong foundation for success and well-being in all areas of your life.

Chapter 19: Parenting Tips for Fostering Social Skills

. . . .

- MODELING POSITIVE Behaviors

Modeling positive behaviors is an essential aspect of promoting positive behavior change in individuals and communities. By demonstrating positive behaviors ourselves, we can inspire and motivate others to follow suit. This modeling of positive behaviors can take place in various contexts, such as at home, in school, in the workplace, and in the community. In this article, we will explore the importance of modeling positive behaviors, as well as some strategies for effectively doing so.

One of the key reasons why modeling positive behaviors is important is that human beings are social creatures who learn by observing and imitating others. This process, known as social learning theory, was popularized by psychologist Albert Bandura in the 1960s. According to Bandura, individuals learn new behaviors by observing others and the consequences of those behaviors. When we model positive behaviors, we provide a clear example for others to follow and show them the benefits of engaging in those behaviors.

Furthermore, modeling positive behaviors can create a positive and supportive environment for behavior change. When individuals see others engaging in positive behaviors, they are more likely to feel encouraged and motivated to do the same. This can create a positive feedback loop where individuals inspire each other to engage in positive behaviors, leading to a culture of positivity and encouragement.

In addition to inspiring others, modeling positive behaviors can also help individuals develop their own skills and abilities. By observing and mimicking positive behaviors, individuals can learn new strategies for coping with challenges, managing stress, and achieving success. This can be particularly beneficial for children and young adults, who are still developing their own behavioral repertoire and can benefit greatly from positive role models.

There are several strategies that can help individuals effectively model positive behaviors. One key strategy is to be consistent in our own behavior. If we want others to follow our example, we need to demonstrate the behaviors we want to see on a regular basis. This consistency can help build trust and credibility with others, making them more likely to emulate our behaviors.

Another important strategy is to communicate our motivations and intentions behind our actions. By explaining why we are engaging in certain behaviors and how they benefit us, we can help others understand the value of those behaviors and motivate them to adopt them as well. This can be particularly important when trying to instill positive behaviors in others, as it helps create a shared understanding and purpose.

To finish, it is important to provide positive reinforcement for those who demonstrate positive behaviors. By acknowledging and rewarding individuals for their efforts, we can encourage them to continue engaging in those behaviors and make them feel valued and appreciated. This can help create a supportive and motivating environment that fosters positive behavior change. By serving as positive role models, we can inspire and motivate others to engage in positive behaviors, create a supportive environment for behavior change, and help individuals develop new skills and abilities. By being consistent in our own behavior, communicating our motivations and intentions, and providing positive reinforcement, we can effectively model positive behaviors and create a culture of positivity and encouragement.

- Creating a Supportive Environment

Creating a supportive environment is essential for cultivating a positive and productive atmosphere in any setting, whether it be in the workplace, at home, or in a classroom. A supportive environment can help individuals feel valued, empowered, and motivated to reach their full potential. It involves fostering a sense of community, respect, and inclusion, where individuals feel safe, understood, and encouraged to express themselves freely without fear of judgment or reprisal. In this essay, we will explore the key components of creating a supportive environment and discuss strategies for promoting an atmosphere of support and collaboration in various contexts.

One of the fundamental aspects of creating a supportive environment is ensuring that all individuals feel accepted and valued for who they are. This requires promoting a culture of respect, empathy, and inclusivity, where diversity is celebrated and differences are seen as strengths rather than obstacles. By acknowledging and appreciating the unique perspectives and backgrounds of each individual, we can create a sense of belonging and foster a spirit of cooperation and collaboration. This can be achieved through open communication, active listening, and a willingness to learn from others' experiences and insights. By creating a culture of respect and inclusion, we can build trust and strengthen relationships, leading to a more harmonious and supportive environment for all.

In addition to promoting a culture of respect and inclusion, it is important to provide support and encouragement to individuals to help them thrive and succeed. This can involve offering mentorship, coaching, and guidance to help individuals develop their skills, overcome challenges, and achieve their goals. By offering constructive feedback, recognition, and praise, we can inspire individuals to strive for excellence and take pride in their accomplishments. It is also important to create opportunities for individuals to collaborate, share ideas, and work together towards common goals. This can help individuals feel connected and engaged, fostering a sense of teamwork and camaraderie that can enhance productivity and morale.

Moreover, creating a supportive environment requires fostering a culture of openness, transparency, and trust, where individuals feel comfortable expressing their thoughts, feelings, and concerns without fear of retribution. This can involve creating channels for feedback, dialogue, and conflict resolution, where individuals can voice their opinions and engage in constructive discussions to address issues and find solutions. By creating a safe and supportive space for communication, we can promote a culture of trust and accountability that encourages honesty, integrity, and collaboration. This can help prevent misunderstandings, conflicts, and miscommunication, leading to a more harmonious and productive environment for all.

Furthermore, creating a supportive environment involves promoting a culture of continuous learning, growth, and development, where individuals are encouraged to explore new ideas, acquire new skills, and expand their knowledge and capabilities. This can involve providing access to training, resources, and opportunities for personal and professional development, as well as promoting a growth mindset that encourages individuals to embrace challenges, learn from failures, and persevere in the face of adversity. By fostering a culture of learning and growth, we can empower individuals to take ownership of their personal and professional development, leading to increased confidence, resilience, and adaptability in the face of change and uncertainty. By promoting a culture of respect, empathy, and inclusivity, providing support and encouragement, fostering open communication and trust, and promoting continuous learning and growth, we can create a supportive environment where individuals feel valued, empowered, and motivated to reach their full potential. By embracing these principles and strategies, we can cultivate a culture of support and collaboration that enhances productivity, morale, and well-being for all.

• • • •

- RECAP OF KEY CONCEPTS

As we reflect on the key concepts covered in our previous discussions, it is important to highlight the foundational elements that underpin our understanding of the subject matter. By summarizing and recapping these concepts, we can reinforce our knowledge and build upon it in future studies. Let us revisit these key ideas to solidify our understanding and ensure that we are on the right path towards mastery of the subject.

One of the fundamental concepts that we have explored is the concept of supply and demand. This principle forms the basis of economics and helps us understand how prices are determined in a market economy. The law of demand states that as the price of a good or service increases, the quantity demanded decreases, and vice versa. On the other hand, the law of supply states that as the price of a good or service increases, the quantity supplied increases, and vice versa. This interplay between supply and demand ultimately determines the equilibrium price and quantity in a market.

Another key concept that we have delved into is the concept of elasticity. Elasticity measures the responsiveness of quantity demanded or supplied to changes in price. If a good or service is elastic, a small change in price will lead to a large change in quantity demanded or supplied. On the other hand, if a good or service is inelastic, a change in price will have a minimal effect on quantity demanded or supplied. Understanding elasticity is crucial for businesses to make pricing decisions and for policymakers to implement effective policies.

Market structures are also essential to our understanding of economics. We have explored different types of market structures, ranging from perfect competition to monopoly. In a perfectly competitive market, there are many buyers and sellers, and prices are determined by forces of supply and demand. On the other end of the spectrum, a monopoly exists when a single seller controls the market and sets prices. Understanding these market structures helps us analyze the behavior of firms and predict market outcomes.

In addition to market structures, we have also discussed the role of government intervention in the economy. Governments play a crucial role in regulating markets, providing public goods and services, and redistributing income. Through taxation, subsidies, and regulations, governments can influence the allocation of resources and achieve specific economic objectives. Understanding the impact of government intervention is essential for policymakers and economists to design effective policies that promote economic growth and stability.

Furthermore, we have examined the concept of externalities and public goods. Externalities are the unintended consequences of economic activities that affect third parties. Positive externalities, such as education and healthcare, result in benefits to society beyond the individual participants. On the other hand, negative externalities, such as pollution and traffic congestion, impose costs on society. Public goods, such as national defense and clean air, are non-excludable and non-rivalrous, meaning that individuals cannot be excluded from enjoying the benefits, and one person's consumption does not diminish others' enjoyment.

In summary, we have explored the concept of economic growth and development. Economic growth refers to an increase in the production of goods and services over time, leading to higher standards of living and improved welfare. Development, on the other hand, encompasses broader social, political, and cultural aspects that contribute to overall well-being. Understanding the drivers of economic growth and development is essential for policymakers to implement strategies that foster long-term prosperity and reduce poverty. Supply and demand, elasticity, market structures, government intervention, externalities, public goods, economic growth, and development are critical components that shape our understanding of the economy. As we continue our studies, it is essential to build upon these concepts and apply them to real-world scenarios to analyze and solve complex economic problems. By mastering these key concepts, we can make informed decisions, drive economic progress, and contribute to a more prosperous society.

- Final Thoughts on Raising Remarkable Kids

Raising children is a profound responsibility that comes with its own set of challenges and rewards. As parents, our ultimate goal is to raise remarkable kids who are equipped with the skills and qualities necessary to thrive in an ever-changing world. Throughout their upbringing, we aim to instill values, foster independence, and encourage personal growth. However, the journey of raising remarkable kids is not without its obstacles. It requires dedication, patience, and a willingness to adapt to the needs of each individual child.

One of the key components of raising remarkable kids is setting clear expectations and boundaries. Children thrive in environments where they know what is expected of them and where there are clear consequences for their actions. By establishing consistent rules and routines, parents can help their children develop a sense of responsibility and self-discipline. However, it is important to remember that rules should be age-appropriate and flexible to accommodate the changing needs of each child.

Another important aspect of raising remarkable kids is fostering a positive and nurturing relationship with them. Children learn best when they feel loved, supported, and respected by their parents. By providing a safe and secure environment, parents can help their children develop a strong sense of self-worth and confidence. It is essential to spend quality time with your children, listen to their thoughts and feelings, and show genuine interest in their lives. By building a strong connection with your children, you can help them navigate the challenges of growing up with grace and resilience.

In addition to setting expectations and building strong relationships, parents can also help their children develop important life skills that will serve them well in the future. Teaching children the value of hard work, perseverance, and resilience can help them overcome obstacles and achieve their goals. By encouraging them to take on responsibilities, set goals, and face challenges head-on, parents can help their children develop a strong work ethic and a growth mindset. It is important to provide opportunities for children to learn new skills, explore their interests, and take on leadership roles. By empowering children to take ownership of their lives and pursue their passions, parents can help them become confident, capable, and successful individuals.

As parents, it is crucial to model the behavior and values that you want to instill in your children. Children learn by example, so it is important to demonstrate kindness, respect, and integrity in all aspects of your life. By showing empathy, compassion, and understanding towards others, parents can teach their children the importance of treating others with dignity and respect. It is also important to model healthy habits and behaviors, such as good communication, problem-solving skills, and self-care practices. By embodying these qualities yourself, you can inspire your children to emulate these positive traits and behaviors in their own lives. By setting clear expectations, fostering positive relationships, teaching important life skills, and modeling positive behavior, parents can help their children develop into confident, capable, and compassionate individuals. It is important to remember that each child is unique and may require different approaches and strategies to support their individual growth and development. By remaining open-minded, adaptable, and supportive, parents can create a nurturing environment where their children can flourish and thrive. By investing time and effort into raising remarkable kids, parents can help shape the future generations and make a positive impact on the world.